fun with
GARDENING

fun with
GARDENING

CLARE BRADLEY

PHOTOGRAPHY BY JOHN FREEMAN

50 GREAT PROJECTS KIDS CAN PLANT THEMSELVES

southwater

This edition is published by Southwater

Distributed in the UK by
The Manning Partnership
251–253 London Road East
Batheaston
Bath BA1 7RL
UK
tel. (0044) 01225 852 727
fax (0044) 01225 852 852

Distributed in Australia by
Sandstone Publishing
Unit 1, 360 Norton Street
Leichhardt
New South Wales 2040
Australia
tel. (0061) 2 9560 7888
fax (0061) 2 9560 7488

Distributed in New Zealand by
Five Mile Press NZ
PO Box 33-1071
Takapuna
Auckland 9
New Zealand
tel. (0064) 9 4444 144
fax (0064) 9 4444 518

Southwater is an imprint of Anness Publishing Limited
© 1996, 2000 Anness Publishing Limited

1 3 5 7 9 10 8 6 4 2

Publisher: Joanna Lorenz
Project Editor: Joanne Rippin
Designer: Alan Marshall
Photographer: John Freeman
Stylist: Judy Williams
Illustrator: Andrew Tewson

The author and publishers would like to thank Ben and Nick Coggins, Shyamoli
Burman-Roy, Nicola Hewitt, Thomas and Sam Mikkelson,
Claudius Hotobah-During, Leslie Wilson, Rosemary and Hugh Lobley, Alka Savani, Karly Robinson,
Charlotte Rawling, Babak Eslamian, David Alexander Heravi, Jennifer Kirkham, Zoe Whittaker,
Griff Williams and Joel Ainsworth for appearing in this book.

Previously published as *Step-by-step Gardening Projects for Kids*

CONTENTS

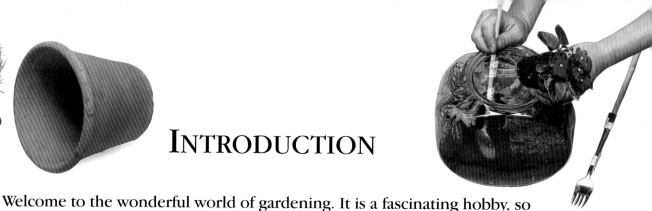

INTRODUCTION

Welcome to the wonderful world of gardening. It is a fascinating hobby, so watch out! It is easy to get hooked. There is a great big world out there that is full of interesting plants, and you don't have to be an expert to start growing them – gardening is all about having a go and you will never know if you can grow a plant until you try. You will certainly have some failures – everyone does – but you will also have some great successes, sometimes completely unexpected, and that is what makes it such fun.

There are so many plants to discover, every year you'll find more of your own personal favourites. Last year my mini-pond was a great discovery and twelve months later it is still looking good. My desert garden reminds me of lovely hot, dry, sunny places even in the depths of winter, and when I made the scarecrow my dog was convinced that there was an intruder in the garden so it obviously worked!

While you are having a great time gardening, you are also making a small patch of earth a little greener and more beautiful, which is good for people, wildlife and conservation too. These projects are a good way to start, so choose one and get growing!

Equipment

You don't need lots of fancy equipment and you don't need all these tools to start gardening. For many projects just a trowel and hand fork will do, but as you get more enthusiastic, some of these tools will be very useful.

Bamboo canes
Canes are for staking plants, making a compost bin and a wigwam for climbing plants.

Broom
Gardening can be rather like housework because there is always a lot of tidying up to do.

Buckets
Good for collecting weeds and carrying soil, hand tools or even water.

Potting compost (soil)
This is used for potting house plants. It will feed your plants the nutrients they need.

Fork
For loosening the soil, and adding compost and manure.

Gardening gloves
Use these to protect your hands from thorns and stinging nettles, and to keep them clean. Try to find a pair that fits properly, if they are too big they can be difficult to work in.

Hand fork
For carefully loosening the soil between plants in small flower beds and for window boxes.

Hoe
For weeding. It slices like a knife under the roots of weeds which then shrivel up and die.

Penknife
Often useful instead of scissors.

Rake
For making a level surface.

Scissors
Used mainly for cutting garden twine, but useful for snipping off all sorts of things.

Secateurs (clippers)
For cutting off plant stems and small branches.

Seed tray
Seed trays are used for sowing seeds and growing seedlings.

Spade
For turning over the soil by digging and for making holes for planting trees and shrubs.

Trowel
A mini spade for making small holes and digging up big weeds.

Twine
This is gardening string for tying plants, and for marking out a straight line.

Watering can
A very important piece of equipment as without water plants die quickly. Immediately after planting always water thoroughly with the sprinkler for a gentle rain-like shower.

Wheelbarrow
For carting all sorts of things round the garden.

Wire
Useful for holding plants against walls and fences. Little pieces are used for pegging down.

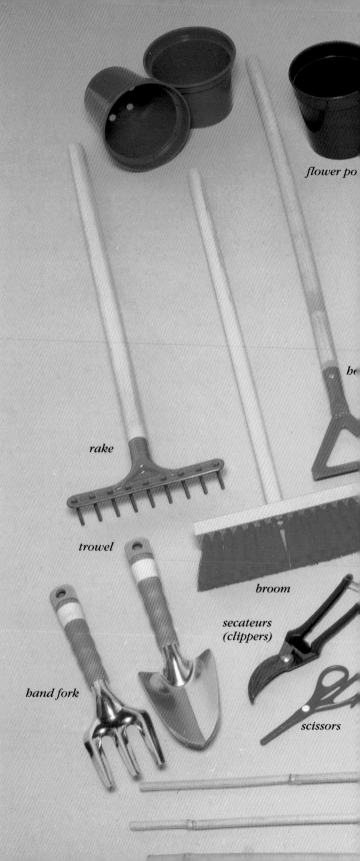

flower po[ts]

rake

trowel

hand fork

broom

secateurs (clippers)

scissors

seed tray

wheelbarrow

spade

wire

buckets

fork

gloves

compost

twine

penknife

watering can

bamboo canes

Weed-out

Weeds are very clever and successful plants which make the most of every opportunity that comes their way. Some, such as dandelions and alkanet, have very long, fleshy roots that can grow from the smallest piece left in the ground. Others, such as bindweed, have tough leathery roots that snake through the soil, and twining stems which grow so quickly that they take over everything in sight.

LONG-LIVED WEEDS
You have to work really hard to get rid of these. Dig right down into the soil using a spade or trowel to get out as much root as you can.

Nettle
Everyone knows this plant because of its stinging hairs, but did you know that there are two types? The smaller one lives for only a short time and has white roots, while the larger one lives for several years, and has spreading stems that creep along the soil and roots that are yellow. The smaller one can easily be pulled up using gloves, but the larger one needs a little more patience to dig up the long roots and creeping stems. Watch out, they both sting!

Bindweed
This is a real nuisance because it can regrow from just the tiniest piece of root left in the soil. It climbs with twining stems that choke out everything else.

Alkanet
This weed has pretty blue flowers but it is a bully in a flower bed, and will eventually take over. It has a long, thick tap root like a dandelion so it is difficult to dig out.

Dandelion
You have to dig deep to get this one out because it can make a new plant from the smallest piece left in the soil. The well-known dandelion "clock" is the seed head which gets blown about by the wind.

Many of these can be pulled out by hand or, using a hoe, by chopping off the roots and leaving the tops to shrivel and die. These are weeds spread by seeds, so catch them before they flower and do more damage.

Oxalis

This has very pretty flowers, but don't be fooled, it is one of the most difficult weeds to get rid of. It grows from small bulbils growing underground, which must be dug up and carefully thrown away. Don't put them on the compost heap, otherwise you will spread them around even more.

Sow thistle

The best way to get rid of this in flower and vegetable beds is to hoe it or pull it up. The seeds are very light and have a plume of hairs which carries them in the wind. If you break the stem, it has a milky juice.

Mercury

Another weed that quickly seeds itself almost anywhere, but it can easily be pulled up or hoed off.

Groundsel

This seems to pop up everywhere, but at least it is easy to pull up. Try and catch it before it makes seeds.

Plantain

Often found in lawns where its large, flat rosettes hug the ground to escape the mower's blades. It is quite tough but can usually be pulled out by hand.

Shepherd's purse

A little weed that is very quick-growing. It has triangular seeds which get sticky when wet and can be carried around on boots and tools. Each plant can produce up to 4,000 seeds in one year that can survive in the soil for up to 30 years!

Glossary

Bulb
Some plants have an underground part that is specially adapted for storing food and protecting the start of a shoot. A dry bulb is a resting plant, as soon as it has some water and something to grow in, roots will grow from the bottom and a shoot from the top.

Cloche (bell jar)
This is a cover that is put over tender plants to protect them from the weather. The simplest one is the top half of a plastic bottle (with the top removed so that air can get in).

Compost
There are different sorts of compost. Potting compost (soil) is used to grow plants in, and also for seed sowing. It is better than soil because it is carefully made to a recipe that makes sure it holds air, water and plant food. Buy peat-free compost if you can, to protect threatened peat bogs. Garden compost is made from recycled vegetable and fruit peelings and tea leaves and garden clippings. All the ingredients are heaped together in a compost bin where after a few months they turn into rich compost that is full of goodness, perfect for digging into beds.

Cutting
A cutting is a piece of a plant stem, usually the tip, that when planted will make its own roots and grow into another plant.

Drainage
Water, whether it is rain or from a watering can, is used by plants as it passes through the soil. The water that doesn't get used must be able to escape from the soil, or drain away, otherwise the plant's roots become water-logged and the plant dies. Flower pots must always have holes in the bottom, and garden soil should be forked over occasionally to help any excess water drain away.

Earthing up
When you are growing potatoes you need to cover up the first shoots with soil or potting compost. This is called earthing up and it encourages the stems to make more potatoes and stops light getting to them. Light turns potatoes green which is slightly poisonous.

Fertile
A fertile soil is one that is in good condition and holds lots of food for plants.

Fertilizer
Fertilizer is food for plants. There are many different sorts in granules, powders or liquids. It will say on the packet which type of plant it is for. Buy organic fertilizer whenever you can, chemical ones can be toxic.

Flower
The flower is the part of a plant from which the fruit or seed will develop. They are usually brightly-coloured to attract the insects which pollinate them.

Germination
When a seed starts to grow, it germinates by growing leaves and stems.

Leaf
Leaves are used by plants to catch food. Green leaves trap sunlight and carbon dioxide from the air and turn it into sugars for energy to grow. In return, they give back oxygen to the air which all animals need.

Manure
Manure is made from the straw bedding of horses or cattle, it has all their droppings mixed in with it. It isn't smelly at all, because the animals only eat grass which decomposes naturally and is full of goodness. Manure is forked into flower beds and put in the bottom of planting holes and is an excellent fertilizer.

Pinching out
Pinching out is removing the top pair of leaves from the stem tip; this makes a plant grow bushy rather than tall and thin.

Pollen
The fine, yellow dust which you see inside a flower is called pollen. It is usually collected by bees from the stamens – which are the male part of the flower – and carried to the female part of another flower (the stigma), this is called pollination.

Pricking out (thinning)
When seeds germinate they are usually growing close together and need to be moved into a bigger pot where they have more room to grow. This is normally done when they have three or four leaves, it is called pricking out (thinning).

Rootball
This is the area immediately around the base of the plant where there are lots of feeding roots. It gets bigger as the plant grows.

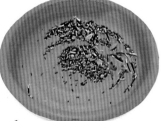

Runner
Some plants, like strawberries, make long stems that creep over the soil. When they find an empty spot, the stem will make roots and eventually grow into a new plant.

Secateurs (clippers)
Tough gardeners' scissors that can be used for cutting thick plant stems.

Seed
Seeds are like tiny time-capsules, they can rest for years, carrying a minute package of information and energy which will grow into a new plant when water and soil are added.

Seed bed
A seed bed is a piece of soil that has been prepared for planting seeds, with a firm, level surface.

Seed drill
A seed drill is a groove in the soil into which seeds are sown.

Shrub
A shrub is a bush that will live for many years.

Soil
The soil is the top layer of earth in which plants grow. It is made from tiny particles of rocks, which have been worn down over millions of years, mixed with minute bits of dead plants.

Sowing
When you put seeds into the soil to grow you are sowing them. You can sow seeds directly into the soil, or into seed trays to keep on your windowsill. Remember to water thoroughly whenever you sow some seeds.

Stake
A stake is a stout, strong stick that is used to support a plant and stop it falling over or growing the wrong way.

Stem
The part of the plant that is above the ground and carries the leaves and flowers is called the stem.

Weed
A weed is any plant that is growing somewhere you don't want it to be. They are usually plants that grow very fast and if you leave them, they take over.

Soil care

Soil is made from bits of rock and all sorts of plant and animal remains. It is wonderful stuff and without it, no plants could grow and no people or animals could survive, so it is worth taking care of!

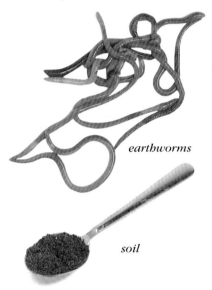

earthworms

soil

HEALTHY SOIL

Healthy soil is teaming with wildlife. Many animals are so small that you cannot see them. In fact there are billions of busy minute animals in every teaspoonful of soil.

Earthworms and beetles are appreciated for their good work. They create tunnels that allow air and water in, and surplus water to drain out. They eat loads of leaves and bits of plants, and turn them into very rich compost which is food for plants.

The soil is a living thing and, like the plants growing in it and all other living things, it needs looking after.

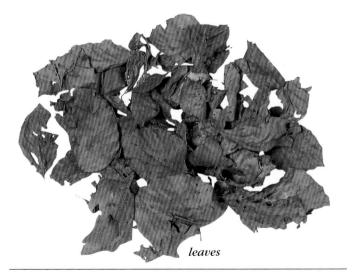

leaves

leaf mould

DIGGING AND FORKING

Digging and forking the soil lets in air which is important for the plants' roots and for all the animals living in the soil. Never work on the soil when it is wet because it can turn into mud without any air. Dig or fork the soil by turning it over down to a depth of about 30 cm (12 in). Break up all the large lumps but leave the surface level.

When you are gardening, try not to walk on the soft soil around your plants, because that squashes out the air too.

manure

Fertilizers contain plant foods, and there are many different sorts that come in the form of granules, powders or liquids. It always says clearly on the packet the type of plant it should be used for and how you should apply it.

compost

fertilizer

A mulch is a thick layer of manure or garden compost, which is put on the surface of the soil around plants. In a year's time it will have virtually disappeared, but in the meantime it has fed and conditioned the soil and stopped any weeds growing.

THE MAGIC OF MANURE AND COMPOST

The soil, like every living thing, needs feeding. In nature leaves fall and plants and animals die and decay. In the garden we need to add manure, compost and fertilizers.

Manure is rotted-down bedding and droppings from animals like horses and cows that have a vegetarian diet. It is wonderful stuff for the soil because it helps to hold water and keeps the soil loose. It is also very rich in plant foods.

If you don't have any farms or stables near you, garden compost is just as good as manure and is something everyone can make. Use some sort of container to collect vegetable peelings from the kitchen, and prunings and soft weeds from the garden. Piled into a heap, they rot down in a few months, making stuff that looks like soil but is a feast for all kinds of plants.

Use manure and garden compost to fork into the soil and into planting holes. For perfect plants and to save on weeding, pile as much as you can around the plants after planting. This is called a mulch and is the best gift of all for soil and plants.

Sowing seeds indoors

Many plants that are grown for their summer flowers come from warm parts of the world. To grow them in countries with colder climates, they have to be started off indoors and only planted outside when there are no more frosts.

GARDENER'S TIP
Don't forget to write the name of the seeds on a label and stick it in so that you don't forget what you've planted.

YOU WILL NEED
seed or potting compost (soil)
seed tray
small flower pot with flat bottom
seeds
shallow seed tray

shallow seed tray

seed tray

seeds

potting compost (soil)

flower pot

1 Use seed or potting compost (soil) to fill a seed tray. Overfill it, then knock the compost (soil) level and use a small pot with a flat bottom to press the surface down slightly to level it all over.

2 Sow the seeds, spacing them out carefully with about 1 cm (½ in) between each seed.

3 Cover the seeds with a little compost (soil), just enough so you cannot see them any more.

4 To water the seeds without disturbing them, stand the seed tray in a shallow seed tray of water so it soaks the compost (soil) up from the bottom. Add a little water at a time, when the compost (soil) is wet enough, it will feel heavy and you will see the moisture glistening on the surface.

Pricking out (thinning)

When seeds have germinated and grown a few leaves, they need to be moved so they can be given space to grow bigger.

YOU WILL NEED
small flower pot
potting compost (soil)
small stick
watering can

watering can

flower pot

stick

potting compost (soil)

1 Fill a small pot with compost (soil). Level and firm it lightly.

2 With one hand use a small stick to lever the seedling out of the compost (soil), and hold the seedling by a seed leaf with the other.

3 Move the seedling to the pot and use the stick to make a hole, which should be deep enough for the roots to fit in comfortably.

4 Place the seedling in the hole and press some potting compost (soil) lightly against the roots. Be very careful, they are very delicate. Water in, using a watering can with a sprinkler on the end to give a gentle shower.

DID YOU KNOW?

The first pair of leaves at the bottom are called the seed leaves. They usually look different from the others and are used by the young seedlings to give them the first boost of energy to get growing.

Making a seed bed

A seed bed is easy to make when you know how and have had a bit of practice. It is important to make it as level as possible so that the tiny seeds can reach the small soil particles to get food and water as soon as possible.

YOU WILL NEED
spade or fork
rake
bamboo cane
short stick
seeds

bamboo cane

spade

rake

stick

seeds

1 Use a spade or fork to turn over the soil, working in a straight line. Knock out any large lumps and take out any weeds and stones as you go.

2 To get a level surface, the soil needs to be firm. Do a duck walk up and down, pressing in with your heels on the forked-over soil.

3 Use a rake to make it level. Pull it gently backwards and forwards, and flick out any remaining stones.

Sowing outside

Some plants need to be sown indoors because they are not hardy enough to grow outside. Others can be sown straight into the ground, but read the packet to make sure you are sowing at the right time of the year. To sow outside, you need to make a seed drill.

GARDENER'S TIP
Don't forget to write a label and stick it in at the end of the row.

1 To make a seed drill, put something with a straight edge (like a bamboo cane) onto the prepared soil. Then use a short stick to mark out a groove against it, about 2 cm (¾ in) deep.

2 Place large seeds into the drill, at least 1 cm (½ in) apart. Small seeds should be sprinkled evenly pinch-by-pinch on a day when there isn't much wind.

3 Cover them over with soil by hand and pat it down gently.

4 When you have covered all the seeds, water thoroughly with the sprinkler on your watering can. Make sure the water comes out gently or you will move the seeds in their bed.

Bugs: the good, the bad and the ugly

Bugs can be gardeners' friends as well as enemies, so it is important to recognize the good guys like ladybird and lacewing larvae, as well as the baddies.

Here are some of the most common and important bugs which you will find in your garden. Encourage the insects which are on your side to stay by creating the right environment for them. Don't be frightened of them! They're much smaller than you and each one has an important role to play in the life of a garden.

Examine your garden for these insects and find out who lives where.

THE GOOD

Butterfly and bee tub.

Bees
Without bees we would have hardly any fruit or vegetables because they play the vital role of pollinating the flowers.

Beetles
Beetles scurry around at night feeding on the small insects and slugs that feed on your plants.

Lacewings
These pretty insects have see-through lacy wings, and the larvae feed on plant-eating greenflies (aphids).

Ladybirds
Both the ladybird itself and its larvae feed greedily on greenfly (aphids) and help to keep them under control.

Encourage lacewings to stay in your garden by making them somewhere to live.

THE BAD

Caterpillars
Caterpillars feed hungrily on all sorts of plants. If they are on your cabbages, you might want to get rid of them. However, many caterpillars are fascinating to watch and they do turn into beautiful moths and butterflies.

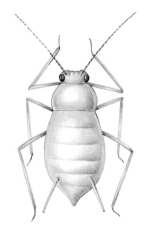

Greenflies (aphids)
Greenflies (aphids) have pointed mouths with which they pierce the leaves and stems of plants and suck out the sap. The plants then become misshapen and weak.

A blast of water will help to reduce the numbers – soapy water is best. The trouble with a lot of chemical sprays is that they kill all the good guys too, who would normally help to keep the greenflies (aphids) under control.

Slugs
Slugs are a problem for gardeners. They love to graze hungrily on succulent seedlings that we have carefully been cultivating and they leave a tell-tale silvery trail behind.

The best way to control them is to go out at night when they are feeding, pick them off and drop them in a pot of salty water. Or buy some slug pellets.

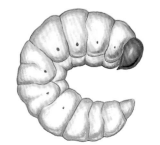

Vine weevil
This is a baddie, no doubt about it! The adult weevil lives a secretive life feeding on the leaves of plants, but it is their larvae that do the real damage.

They feed off the roots of plants, usually of those growing in pots and containers although they can sometimes be found in flower beds too.

Plants being attacked start to wilt, then topple over as soon as you touch them because they have no roots left. If you find any, immediately throw away all the compost or soil that the affected plant was growing in.

THE UGLY

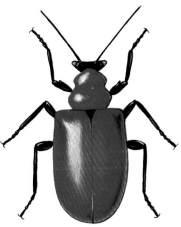

Lily beetle
Lily beetles are often left alone because they are a pretty bright red colour. Their larvae, however, are one of the ugliest things around. They are covered in a horrible jelly-like mucus which protects them.

Both the adult beetles and the larvae feed on lily leaves and stems and can quickly strip a plant so watch out for them!

A Bag of Potatoes

Home-grown potatoes taste ten times better than bought ones, and nothing could be easier to grow. Start them off early in the year using potatoes either from your vegetable rack at home, or, better still, using special seed potatoes from a garden centre. When the plant starts flowering the potatoes are ready for harvesting. This is about 10-12 weeks after planting.

YOU WILL NEED
seed potatoes
egg box
strong, dark coloured plastic bag
potting compost (soil)
sharp object to make holes in bag

potting compost (soil)

screwdriver

egg box

seed potatoes

plastic bag

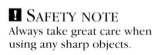

! SAFETY NOTE
Always take great care when using any sharp objects.

1 To help your potatoes get off to a speedy start, put them in an egg box with the end that has the most eyes pointing upwards. This is where the baby shoots will grow from. Place the box on a cool but light windowsill and leave for a few weeks until the first signs of life appear – little fat green leaves.

2 Fill the plastic bag one-third full of potting compost (soil), and make a few holes with a screwdriver in the bottom so that excess water can drain through.

3 Plant 2 or 3 potatoes in the bag, with their shoots pointing upwards.

4 Cover them over with potting compost (soil) so you end up with the bag half full. Give the bag a good water and put it outside, in a sheltered place where it will not get caught by a frost.

5 After several weeks when the shoots are between 15 and 30 cm (6 and 12 in) tall, add more compost (soil) so the bag is completely full. This is called earthing up and it encourages the stems to make more potatoes as well as stopping light getting to them.

DID YOU KNOW?
Sunlight makes potatoes go green and green potatoes are poisonous to eat – enough to give you an upset tummy.

A Sunny Spot and a Shady One

There is a plant for every place in the garden and neither bright sun nor a bit of shade is any problem. Here are two little gardens, one for the sun and one for the shade.

A SUNNY SPOT

Hot dry places are not ideal for every plant but some, like marigolds, petunias and cosmeas (cosmos), absolutely love it. Grey-leafed plants like cotton lavender, usually come from warm countries and always do well in hot sunny places. Follow steps 1 and 2 for a shady spot to prepare the ground for this sunny garden.

YOU WILL NEED
trowel
cosmeas (cosmos)
cotton lavender or other grey-
 leaved plant
petunias
marigolds

marigold   *cosmeas (cosmos)*

petunias   *trowel*

1 When you have prepared the ground plant the cosmea seedlings at the back. They grow over a metre (3 feet) tall so they need the most space.

2 Plant the cotton lavender, which has lovely yellow flowers in early summer, in front of the cosmeas (cosmos).

3 Plant the petunias and marigolds in the front of the bed. Water thoroughly.

GARDENER'S TIP
Be sure to take off all the faded marigold and petunia flowers before they make seeds, that way they will dazzle you with colour for months.

A SHADY SPOT

All sorts of plants will flourish in a shady flower bed, but for colour all summer long, it is difficult to beat a combination of fuchsias and busy lizzies (patience plants). You could also use primroses, lilies and ferns.

YOU WILL NEED
compost or fertilizer
trowel
fuchsia
busy lizzies
 (patience plants)
woodruff seeds

fuchsia

*busy lizzies
(patience plants)*

*woodruff
seeds*

trowel

1 Get rid of any weeds by pulling them out or hoeing off.

2 Fork over the soil and give it a boost by forking in a generous helping of good garden compost or manure, or a handful of fertilizer.

3 Start by planting the tallest plant, the fuchsia, at the back. Use a trowel to dig a hole that is slightly deeper than the pot, ease the fuchsia out of its pot and plant it in the hole.

4 Plant the busy lizzies (patience plants) around the fuchsia, spacing them about 20 cm (8 in) apart. Sprinkle the woodruff seeds in the gaps. Water the garden thoroughly.

Cunning Cuttings

Early in the year, fresh young shoots are bursting with energy and can be cut off and persuaded to make roots. Try taking cuttings of lots of different plants – some are easier than others but you won't know until you try.

YOU WILL NEED
small shallow flower pot
potting compost (soil)
penknife or scissors
fuchsia
plastic bag
piece of string

fuchsia

flower pot

potting compost (soil)

piece of string

penknife

plastic bag

DID YOU KNOW?
The plastic bag helps to keep the air moist around the leaves, while the cuttings make roots to grow away on their own.

⚠ SAFETY NOTE
Always take great care when using any sharp objects.

1 Fill a small shallow flower pot either with ordinary (regular) potting compost (soil) or, even better, one that is specially mixed for cuttings.

3 Gently take off the lower pair of leaves, being careful not to tear the stem.

2 Using a penknife or scissors, cut off a shoot tip which is at least 5 cm (2 in) long and which has three sets of leaves

from the fuchsia. Then make a clean, straight cut just below where a pair of leaves joins the stem.

4 Make a hole in the compost (soil) and put the cutting in. Then press the compost (soil) lightly against the stem. Fill the pot with a few more cuttings, spacing them about 3 cm (1½ in) apart.

GARDENER'S TIP
If you don't have any potting compost (soil), it is often possible to root cuttings in a glass of water. After a couple of weeks in one pot the cuttings will need more space and should be gently moved to pots of their own.

5 Give the pot a good watering then put it in a plastic bag and tie the top together with string. Place on a light windowsill and watch a new plant grow!

Good Enough to Eat!

You don't need a large garden to grow fruit and vegetables – it is possible to grow some in just a window box. Strawberries and bush or trailing types of tomatoes are small enough, so are radishes and lettuces.

YOU WILL NEED
window box
potting compost (soil)
tomato plants
strawberry plants
radish seeds
lettuce seeds
nasturtium seeds

GARDENER'S TIP
To get a plant out of a pot, turn it upside down with the stem between your fingers. With the other hand, firmly squeeze the bottom of the pot to loosen it.

DID YOU KNOW?
Nasturtium leaves and flowers are edible, with a hot, peppery taste. They look lovely on a plate of salad.

window box

strawberry plants

potting compost (soil)

tomato plants

nasturtium seeds

lettuce seeds

radish seeds

1 Fill the window box with potting compost (soil) to just below the rim.

2 Plant the tomatoes in the back corners of the window box.

3 Plant the strawberries about 30 cm (12 in) away from the tomatoes.

4 Sow radish and lettuce seeds 1 cm (½ in) apart The radishes will come first, then the lettuces can have the space.

5 Sow some nasturtium seeds in the corners so that they can grow up and trail over the edge. Water thoroughly.

The Tallest Sunflower

Sunflowers are one of the speediest plants to grow in your garden. In just 6 months they outstrip everything else and can easily grow up to 3 metres (10 ft) tall.

They need some sort of support to stop them blowing over in windy weather. Plant them against a wall or fence that you can tie them to, or use a tall bamboo cane.

YOU WILL NEED
small flower pot
potting compost (soil)
sunflower seeds
watering can
a very tall bamboo cane – at least
  2 m (6 ft)
string

flower pots   *sunflower seeds*

*potting compost
(soil)*

bamboo canes

string

1 Fill the flower pots with compost (soil) and sow 2 or 3 seeds about 1 cm (¹/₂ in) deep. Water them in using a watering can with a sprinkler on the end.

2 When the seeds have germinated, pull out all but the strongest seedling in each pot.

3 Keep the pots on a sunny window sill until the seedlings have grown and the weather is warm, then plant outside.

4 Put the cane in the soil and tie it loosely to the plant. Measure the height of the plant when the flower appears.

Lovely Lilies

Few flowers have as much going for them as lilies. They are exotic, colourful and often heavily scented. They are also easy to grow and are perfect for planting in pots. Be sure to buy only fat, healthy bulbs with thick, fleshy roots.

YOU WILL NEED
pebbles
large flower pot
potting compost (soil)
3 lily bulbs

potting compost (soil)

flower pot

pebbles

lily bulbs

1 Put a layer of pebbles in the bottom of a large flower pot so that water can drain away easily.

2 Fill the pot half full with potting compost (soil).

GARDENER'S TIP
When the flowers die cut them off. Let the leaves die and in autumn (fall) replant the bulbs into fresh compost and they will grow all over again!

3 Plant the lily bulbs, taking great care of the roots, and spacing the bulbs evenly in the pot.

4 Cover with compost (soil), finishing a little way below the rim of the pot, then water them well.

Wigwam Runners

Runner beans are climbing plants and need something to run up, so a wigwam is just the thing. This looks just as good in a flower bed as in a vegetable garden. The flowers are pretty and are followed by long, tasty beans which, if you pick them every few days, will grow all summer.

YOU WILL NEED
fork
manure or garden compost
5 x 2 m (6 ft) bamboo canes
garden string
runner bean seeds

garden string

runner bean seeds

bamboo canes

compost

DID YOU KNOW?

Runner beans came from the tropical parts of America, so it is no surprise that they like their roots to be in warm soil. They also grow fast – you could have a plate of beans in just 7 weeks!

1 At the end of spring, when the days are warm and there are no more frosts, fork over a patch of soil. Add a bucketful of manure or well-rotted garden compost and mix it in well.

2 Push 5 long bamboo canes into the ground, in a circle measuring roughly 1 m (3 ft) across the middle.

3 Gather the canes together at the top and tie with a piece of string to make a wigwam shape.

4 Plant a seed about 3 cm (1¼ in) deep on both sides of each cane. Water thoroughly. They will soon germinate and start to run up the canes. When they reach the top, pinch out the top few centimetres (inches) of the stem.

Tomatoes in a Bag

Grow-bags are great for growing tomatoes in because they provide almost everything the plant needs. You can buy the bags in most garden centres. The plastic funnel acts as a mini reservoir and makes watering and feeding much easier.

YOU WILL NEED
scissors
1 grow-bag
3 tomato plants
2 bamboo canes
garden twine
large plastic bottle

plastic bottle

tomato plant

garden twine

scissors

grow-bag

bamboo canes

❗ SAFETY NOTE
Always take great care when using any sharp objects.

1 Make drainage holes in the bottom of the grow-bag and cut out the squares marked in the plastic by the dotted lines. Make a hole in each square and plant one of the tomato plants.

2 Push a bamboo cane into each square and tie the plant to it loosely.

3 Cut the bottom off the plastic bottle to make a funnel shape. Plant the funnel next to the plant and fill with water.

DID YOU KNOW?
Tall-growing types of tomato should only be allowed to develop one main stem. Lots of side shoots will try to grow in between where the leaves meet the main stem, and these should be picked off as soon as you spot them.

side shoot

GARDENER'S TIP
Keep the tomatoes well watered and as soon as flowers appear, feed once a week as well with a special tomato fertilizer that is high in potassium which is important for all fruits.

Blooming Old Boots

Don't these look great? It is a blooming wonderful way to recycle an old pair of boots, the bigger the better. It just goes to show that almost anything can be used to grow plants in as long as it has a few holes in the bottom for drainage. Try an old football, a sports bag, or even an old hat, for plant containers with lots of character.

! SAFETY NOTE
Always take great care when using any sharp objects.

YOU WILL NEED
knife
old pair of working boots
potting compost (soil)
selection of bedding plants
watering can

knife

bedding plants

watering can

potting compost (soil)

old boot

1 Using a knife very carefully (in fact you will probably need help), make some holes in between the stitching of the sole for drainage. Even better if there are holes there naturally!

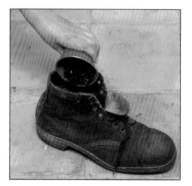

2 Fill the boots with potting compost (soil), pushing it down right into the toe.

3 Plant flowers that can cope with hot, dry places like geraniums and verbenas which will trail over the edge.

5 The boot needs watering every day in the summer, and blooms even better if you mix some plant food in to the water once a week.

4 Squeeze in a pansy with a contrasting flower colour, and a trailing lobelia plant. Lobelia grows in the smallest of spaces and will delicately tumble over the edge.

Sprouting Seeds

How do you grow fresh vegetables at any time of the year without having a garden? Sprouting seeds. They grow quickly, are very good for you and taste delicious too, so who could ask for more? These bean sprouts are grown from mung beans, but other dried seeds like chickpeas (garbanzo beans) and whole lentils work well too. For the quickest results try tiny alfalfa seeds. All these are easy to buy from any health food shop and many supermarkets.

1 Wash the beans and soak them overnight in cold water.

2 Next morning, cover a flat-bottomed dish with a layer of cotton wool, or several sheets of kitchen paper towels, and water.

YOU WILL NEED
flat-bottomed dish
cotton wool or kitchen paper towel
mung beans
newspaper

newspaper

mung beans

flat-bottomed dish

cotton wool

3 Wash the beans again and spread them evenly over the damp bottom of the dish.

4 Cover the dish with newspaper to keep out light and put it in a warm place. The beans will soon sprout and be ready to eat in 6-9 days. Don't let them grow too long, they should be plump and about 2.5 cm (1 in) long for the best taste.

VARIATION

Another way of sprouting larger seeds is to put a large spoonful of dry seeds such as chickpeas (garbanzo beans) into a wide-necked jar and cover with a small piece of muslin (cheesecloth), secured by an elastic band. Fill the jar with water and swish the seeds around a bit, then pour the water out. Do this at least once every day (twice if you can) to stop them going bad. They will take between 2-7 days to sprout, depending on what type you are growing.

DID YOU KNOW?

To cook bean sprouts, wash them, then boil in a pan of salted water for 2 minutes. Drain, and serve with butter and a few drops of soy sauce.

Sweet Sweet Peas

Few flowers smell sweeter than sweet peas. They have a floaty, delicate perfume and an amazing array of colours. The most important thing about growing them is that you must cut the flowers every day to stop seeds developing, that way they will keep flowering for a lot longer. I can think of worse jobs to do, can't you? The seedlings have long, delicate roots so an ideal pot is a long one that is made out of newspaper. It can be planted and left in the soil so the roots are not disturbed.

1 Sweet pea seeds have very hard skins, so soak them overnight in a saucer of water to soften them up.

YOU WILL NEED
sweet pea seeds
small saucer of water
newspaper
stapler
potting compost (soil)
plastic carton
trowel

plastic carton

potting compost (soil)

sweet pea seeds

stapler

newspaper

2 The next morning fold a double sheet of newspaper into 3.

3 Then roll it up to make a tube and staple it together in several places.

4 Hold one hand under one end and fill with potting compost (soil).

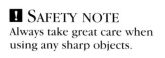

5 Make several tubes and stand them in a plastic carton and plant 3 seeds in each, about 1 cm (½ in) deep. Water them well. Put them outside in a sheltered place or on a shady window-sill. When they are about 10 cm (4 in) tall, pinch out the tip of each stem.

6 Plant them outside in the spring, against some wire netting or canes for them to climb up. Water often.

! SAFETY NOTE
Always take great care when using any sharp objects.

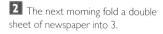

Grow Spaghetti

Yes, it's true! This type of marrow (summer squash) is packed with vegetable spaghetti. It only needs cooking to spill out its treasures. Bake it in the oven, or boil it until soft, add some butter and give it a twirl.

YOU WILL NEED
small flower pot
potting compost (soil)
spaghetti marrow seeds
hand fork
manure or garden compost
trowel
hand fork

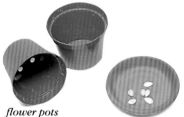

flower pots

spaghetti marrow seeds

potting compost (soil)

DID YOU KNOW?
All marrows (squashes) have separate male and female flowers and to get fruit they need to be pollinated. It is easy to tell which flower is which because the female one always has a swelling at the bottom beneath the petals.

1 Fill a small flower pot with potting compost (soil) and make it level. Plant 3 seeds, pushing them in about 1 cm (½ in) deep.

2 Prepare the soil well, by forking over and adding some manure or garden compost.

3 When the young plant has 3 or 4 fully grown leaves and the weather is nice and warm, plant it outside in the prepared spot.

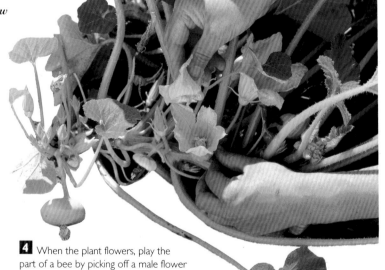

4 When the plant flowers, play the part of a bee by picking off a male flower and dusting the yellow pollen onto the middle of the female one to pollinate it.

5 They are very greedy plants for both water and food. When the first flowers appear, start to add some fertilizer to its water once a week. Choose a fertilizer made especially for flowers and fruit and you will be rewarded with plates piled with vegetable spaghetti.

A Watery World

No garden is complete without the sight and sound of water. Great for toe-dipping on a hot, sunny day, this mini-pond is too small for fish but a welcome watering spot for thirsty birds. Any large container can be used to make a mini-pond, as long as it is watertight! A washing-up (dish washing) bowl is a bit too shallow but would do at a pinch. A toy-tidy, like this one which is deeper, is ideal. So give away some toys and splash in some water instead.

1 Find a large, wide container and put a layer of gravel in the bottom.

2 Fill the container up with water almost to the top.

YOU WILL NEED
large, wide container
gravel
2 aquatic plants like golden sedge
 and monkey flower
lead from a wine bottle top
strands of oxygenating weed
flower pot
potting compost (soil)
small floating plants

3 Lower the aquatic plants (which should already be in net pots when you buy them) gently into the water around the edge of the container.

4 Attach a piece of lead from a wine bottle top round the base of pieces of oxygenating weed to weigh them down.

5 Pot the bunch into an ordinary (regular) flower pot and put a layer of gravel on the surface.

6 Sink the pot into the mini-pond, then add a few floaters like water lettuce and floating ferns. Plant your pond in a hole in the garden so that it keeps cool.

container

aquatic plants

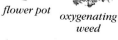

floating plants

flower pot

oxygenating weed

lead

gravel

Turn Detective

Watch out! Be careful where you step. There is a fascinating, hidden world going on unnoticed right beneath your feet. Take time to look and you will be amazed what there is to discover on a mini safari in a garden.

YOU WILL NEED
string
2 bamboo canes or sticks
magnifying glass
notebook and pencil

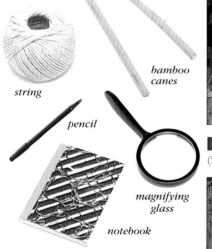

string

bamboo canes

pencil

magnifying glass

notebook

1 Tie a piece of string about 1.5 m (5 ft) long to 2 bamboo canes or sticks.

2 Peg this down across some long grass or a woodland edge.

3 Creep along the line of string very slowly, centimetre by centimetre, (inch by inch) with your nose to the ground looking through a magnifying glass.

4 Try to identify what you find with the help of nature books, or start a nature diary to make notes in.

A Wild One

Native plants are those that have grown naturally in the countryside for thousands of years. Some of the most colourful ones are cornfield flowers, but many are quite rare now. To enjoy them this summer, grow a pot full of wild flowers to stand on your doorstep.

YOU WILL NEED
pebbles
very large flower pot
garden soil
packet of wild flower seeds

flower pot

garden soil

pebbles

wild flower seeds

1 Put a few pebbles in the bottom of the pot for drainage.

2 Fill the pot with garden soil, taking out any bits of roots or large stones.

GARDENER'S TIP
Don't forget to keep watering as the flowers grow! Pots need much more watering than beds because the water drains away.

3 Make sure the surface is level, then sprinkle a large pinch of flower seeds evenly on top.

4 Cover the seeds lightly with soil, just so you can't see them any more, and water them in with a gentle sprinkle.

Garden with a Buzz

To encourage beautiful butterflies and buzzing bees into your garden, grow a few of their favourite plants to tempt them in from miles around. Many butterflies are now becoming scarce, so every butterfly-friendly plant that you can grow will help them to survive. Bees and butterflies like lots of sunshine so put your buzzy garden in a sunny spot.

You WILL NEED
pebbles
a large planter or half barrel
potting compost (soil) or equal
  quantities of garden soil and
  potting compost (soil)
a selection of suitable plants such as
  phlox, aster, lavender, angel's
  pincushion, verbena, blue lobelia
trowel

half barrel

plants

pebbles

1 Put a few pebbles in the bottom of the barrel or planter for drainage, then fill with compost or an equal mixture of soil and compost.

potting compost and soil

trowel

2 Plant phlox and aster in the middle because they are tallest.

3 Plant lavender, angel's pincushion and verbena around the edge.

DID YOU KNOW?
As bees collect their food, they also do the very important job of pollinating the flower, and so provide us with fruit, like apples and pears.

4 Plant blue lobelia in the front, so it tumbles over the edge. Water the tub.

GARDENER'S TIP
Other friendly plants are: broom, catmint, delphiniums, nasturtiums, oxeye daisy, petunias, primroses, stocks, sweet williams and thrift.

Desert Garden

If you like dreaming of hot, sunny places and plants that are not too much trouble, then cacti and succulents are the plants for you. Keep this desert garden on a sunny windowsill and water it well during the summer but hardly at all in the winter. With this winter rest, a cactus might surprise you with a dazzling display of flowers.

YOU WILL NEED
clay flower pot
pebbles
special cacti compost (soil) or
  potting compost (soil), grit and
  sand
rocks
cacti and succulent plants
strips of folded newspaper
gravel

potting compost (soil)

cacti and succulent plants

newspaper

grit and sand

rocks

flower pot

pebbles

1 Find a container that is not too deep but quite wide at the top – it must have holes for drainage. Put a handful of pebbles in the bottom. Fill the pot with special cacti compost (soil) or mix your own, using equal quantities of potting compost (soil), grit and sand.

2 Position one or two large rocks in the container.

3 Pick the cacti up with strips of folded newspaper to protect yourself from getting pricked, and plant them around the rocks.

4 Cover the surface with gravel. During the spring and summer water like ordinary houseplants, but during the winter water about once a month when the compost (soil) is very dry.

Pots of Herbs

A handful of herbs adds the finishing touch to all sorts of dishes. You can keep this pot anywhere in the garden, on a balcony or even on a window sill, to give you lovely, fresh snippets just when you want them. I have put in a silver and a golden thyme because thyme is one of the best herbs for pots, not growing too large and great for soups and sauces.

YOU WILL NEED
large pot
pebbles
potting compost (soil)
selection of herbs such as curry plant, marjoram, parsley, chives and thyme

herbs

large pot

potting compost (soil)

pebbles

1 Put a good handful of pebbles in the bottom of the pot so water can drain out easily (herbs don't like soggy feet).

GARDENER'S TIP
Larger herbs like mint, rosemary and fennel, are great for the first year, but in the second they will outgrow the pot and swamp anything else in it, so it is really best to give them a pot each. Remember to keep all your herbs well watered but not too soggy.

2 Fill the pot almost full with potting compost (soil). The curry plant is the tallest, so plant that in the middle.

3 Plant the marjoram towards the back because it is the next biggest.

4 Work around the pot planting chives, parsley and thyme. You can start using the herbs as soon as you like!

Lacewing Hotel

Greenflies (aphids) are one of the most serious garden pests, so anything that eats them is very welcome! Lacewing larvae do just that and this little hotel will provide a home for the lacewings over the winter months. They crawl into the cosy gaps made by the corrugated card (cardboard), and stay snug while it is cold. Then in spring they breed, and the larvae grow up in your garden to have a field day feeding on your pests.

YOU WILL NEED
large plastic bottle with top on
scissors
corrugated card (cardboard)
pieces of wire

plastic bottle

scissors

corrugated card (cardboard)   *wire*

❗ SAFETY NOTE
Always take great care when using any sharp objects.

1 Carefully cut the bottom off a plastic bottle using scissors (this can be tricky so you might need help).

2 Cut a long piece of corrugated card (cardboard) and roll it up so that you can fit it into the plastic bottle.

3 Make two small holes opposite each other at the bottom of the bottle.

4 Fix a piece of wire through to stop the card falling out. Twist another piece of wire around the bottle top and hang it on a tree or a bush in your garden. Leave the top on so that rain cannot get in and make the living quarters soggy.

Minty Tea

Sprigs of mint look and taste great in cool summer drinks and mint tea is delicious either hot or cold at any time of the year.

YOU WILL NEED
mint leaves
teapot
boiling water
sugar or honey to taste

mint leaves

teapot

❗ SAFETY NOTE
Always take great care when pouring boiling water.

1 Pick a large handful of mint leaves.

2 Tear the leaves into little pieces.

4 Pour on boiling water and leave to steep for 5 minutes before pouring out to drink immediately, or leave until cool and then chill in the refrigerator. Add a little sugar or honey for a special treat.

GARDENER'S TIP
Mint grows very quickly by long running stems that creep through the soil making new plants along their length. Cut one of these off and plant it in a large pot.

3 Put the leaves into the teapot.

Scrumptious Strawberries

Summer just wouldn't be the same without a bowl of freshly picked, ripe-red, juicy strawberries, lightly sprinkled with sugar and served with ice-cream. They are surprisingly quick and easy to grow and, providing you look after them, you will get free pick-your-own for years to come. A strawberry plant grows several long stems which have baby plants along them. These are called runners and can be potted up to produce plants that will have fruit next year.

YOU WILL NEED
small flower pot
trowel
strawberry plant
secateurs (clippers)
tent peg

strawberry plant

flower pot

secateurs (clippers)

tent peg

1 Fill a small flower pot to the top with garden soil.

2 Choose a long, healthy stem that has a baby strawberry plant starting to grow somewhere along its length. Cut off the stem beyond the baby plant.

3 Position the baby plant in the pot of soil and pin it in place using a tent peg.

4 Push the tent peg out through one of the holes in the bottom of the pot. Then position the pot next to the mother plant and push the peg in to secure it.

GARDENER'S TIP

In a few weeks the baby strawberry will have made its own roots in the pot of soil and the stem joining it to the mother plant can be cut off. Plant the new plant in a place that has been made ready by forking and adding fertilizer, or manure.

Miniature Garden

Even without a garden you can become a great garden designer and make the perfect landscape – only in miniature. It is a lot less work than the real thing and just as much fun.

YOU WILL NEED
deep seed tray or wooden box
potting compost (soil)
foil pie dish
small stones
twigs
raffia
ivy
alpine plants
moss
grit
model garden furniture
plant cuttings
dried flowers

potting compost (soil)

moss

stones *grit*

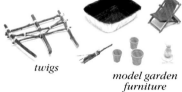

seed tray

foil pie dish

twigs

model garden furniture

1 Fill a seed tray with potting compost, (soil) then start putting in the most permanent features. A foil pie dish makes a great pond and a rockery is easy to make from small stones.

2 Make natural looking fences and trellises from dead twigs, tied together with raffia. Some little pieces of ivy stem look good growing on the fence, it might even take root.

3 Alpine plants are worth investing in if you can. They are perfect because they stay quite small.

5 Use grit to make paths and patios.

4 Use some moss to lay a luxurious lawn. You can find it growing outside in cool, damp places, or you can try growing it yourself by sprinkling a handful of dried moss on the watered surface of a little seed tray.

GARDENER'S TIP

To help the miniature garden to last as long as possible, choose a deep seed tray, a gravel tray or even a strong wooden box. An ordinary (regular) seed tray is fine to start with, but because they are so shallow, the garden will only last for a few weeks.

Keep your miniature garden inside on a cool windowsill or, even better, outside in a sheltered corner and make sure that you keep it watered, at least every day in the summer. These are just some ideas – don't forget the swing, the compost bin, the vegetable patch and the greenhouse made from half a plastic bottle!

6 Add whatever bits and pieces you can find at home to make an assortment of garden furniture and decorations. Finally, fill up the flower beds with dried flowers and little cuttings from any interesting bushes (better ask first).

Time Capsules

Seeds are amazing things – tiny packages that are ready to spring into life when you add water and soil. They are also full of surprises, you could discover a completely new flower from seed you have collected yourself.

DID YOU KNOW?
Most seeds last for a few years, some even last for about 50! Store in envelopes in a cool, dry place over the winter until the spring, or whenever you want to sow them.

YOU WILL NEED
paper bag
newspaper
seed tray
sheet of paper
envelopes
pen

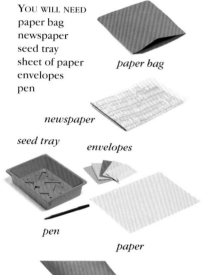

paper bag

newspaper

seed tray

envelopes

pen

paper

1 Only collect seeds on a dry, sunny day and use a paper bag rather than a plastic one to put them in.

2 Put a layer of newspaper in a seed tray and spread out the collected seeds on top. Put them in a dry, warm place for a couple of days to dry thoroughly.

3 Fold a sheet of paper in half, then open out flat so there is just a crease. Rub the seed capsules between your fingers to try and get just the seeds out.

4 Carefully pick out all the bits of stem and seed pods. Blowing lightly can help to remove some of the lighter rubbish.

5 Pour the clean seeds into small envelopes (they should collect in the paper crease which makes it easier to pour them into the envelopes).

6 Don't forget to write the names of the plants on the envelopes – or you will never remember what the seeds are.

Long-lasting Lavender

Need something to make your room smell nice?
Well, I've got just the thing – some good old-
fashioned English lavender. Fill bowls with dried
lavender or make into muslin (cheesecloth) bags
to put among your clothes.

YOU WILL NEED
scissors
fresh lavender
raffia
sheet of paper
small bowl

scissors

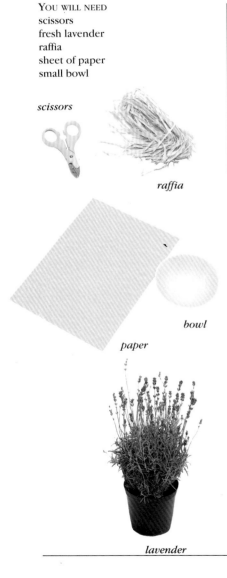

raffia

bowl

paper

lavender

1 Cut whole stalks of lavender when the flowers are showing colour, but are not fully opened.

2 Tie them in small, loose bundles with a bit of raffia.

! SAFETY NOTE
Always take great care when using any sharp objects.

3 Hang them upside down in a warm, dry place for a few days.

4 When the flowers are completely dry, rub them free of the stalks on to a sheet of paper. You can use the lavender to scent rooms or clothes.

Press them Pretty

With a flower press you can keep colourful, summer flowers to cheer you up on a winter's day. A flower press is very easy to make out of things you might just throw away.

YOU WILL NEED
card (cardboard)
scissors
pretty gift wrap
sticky tape
corrugated card (cardboard)
newspaper
ribbon

ribbon

gift wrap

card (cardboard)

newspaper

ated card oard)

adhesive tape

1 Cut out two matching pieces of card any size you like, and cover them with pretty wrapping paper, sticking this down with adhesive tape.

2 Cut out two matching pieces of corrugated card to fit. Because it is crinkled, it lets in the air which slowly dries the flowers.

⚠ SAFETY NOTE
Always take great care when using any sharp objects.

3 Build the press in layers starting with a piece of card (cardboard), then a piece of corrugated card (cardboard) and finally some thick layers of newspaper cut to fit. Lay the flowers on top. Cover with more newspaper and the second sheet of corrugated card (cardboard).

4 Put the remaining piece of cardboard on top. Then tie two pieces of ribbon tightly around, finishing them off with a bow. Keep the press in a warm, airy place for about a week. Your pressed flowers can then be made into birthday cards or pretty pictures.

Scare them off!

Fed up with those pesky pigeons stealing your precious plants? Give them a fright by making a scarecrow out of odds and ends that you find lying around. Model it on someone you know and give them a shock too! My dog would not stop barking at this one, so it certainly works!

YOU WILL NEED
2 sticks – one 1.85 m (6 ft) long, the
 other 1.25 m (4 ft) long
nails
hammer
spade
old pillowcase
permanent marking pen
stuffing: straw, newspapers in
 plastic bags
thick string
safety pins
old clothes

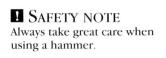

pillowcase *hat*

scarf

shirt *straw stuffing*

1 Put the longer stick on the ground and lay the shorter one across it about 30 cm (12 in) from the top. Nail them together with a couple of nails so that the frame is good and strong. Dig a 30 cm (12 in) hole, plant the frame and fill up the hole with soil.

2 Draw a face on the pillowcase with the open end down. Then bring the top corners together and tie. Fill the pillowcase with stuffing.

3 Put the head over the top of the frame so that the stick goes up into the stuffing. Tie the open end of the pillowcase tightly around the stick with a piece of string. Pin the hat to the head.

4 Tie the trouser bottoms up and fill them with stuffing.

5 Attach the trousers to the frame by running string through the back belt loop and around the stick.

6 Put the shirt on so the ends of the short stick go through the armholes and fill it with stuffing. Now you have a permanent guest in your garden!

 SAFETY NOTE
Always take great care when using a hammer.

Terrific Tyres

Old tyres get a new and completely different lease of life with a lick of paint. They make perfect containers for growing all sorts of plants and are ideal for a first garden.

YOU WILL NEED
coloured emulsion (acrylic) paints
paintbrush
2 tyres
potting compost (soil) and
 garden soil
selection of bedding plants

tyre

paint

paintbrush

*potting compost
and garden soil*

bedding plants

1 Use ordinary emulsion (acrylic) to paint the tyres – any colours look good, the brighter the better.

2 Put one tyre on top of another. Two is deep enough, three would be better for larger plants.

3 Fill them up with potting compost (soil), or equal quantities of garden soil and compost. It takes rather a lot to fill the tyres, so to cut down on the amount, stuff newspaper into the tyres.

4 Put the tallest plants in first – this is a cosmea (cosmos).

5 Surround with smaller plants like geraniums, pansies and marigolds.

GARDENER'S TIP

You can get old tyres for free at most garages. For something cheap and fast-growing, try pumpkin plants. A ring of lobelia will grow happily if planted between the two tyres.

6 Plant some delicate trailing plants to grow over the edge. Start your tyre garden off well by giving it a lot of water. Keep watering through the summer and don't let it get too dry.

Magic Compost

No garden should be without a compost bin. It is a great way to recycle food scraps and turn them into wonderful food for the soil. A few leaves are all right mixed in the compost bin, but in autumn (fall) it is better to collect and compost leaves separately because they take much longer to rot down, normally about 2 years.

YES! – Things to put in
All uncooked vegetable peelings; tea bags; banana and orange skins; apple cores; short-lived weeds; and grass cuttings (never make a thick layer, but mix these in with other things).

NO! – Things to leave out
Any cooked food; tough weeds like dandelions, clover and bindweed; evergreen leaves; sticks; and tough stems.

YOU WILL NEED
wire or plastic netting 1.5 m (5 ft) long
string
4 bamboo canes
newspaper
scissors
card (cardboard)
plastic bag

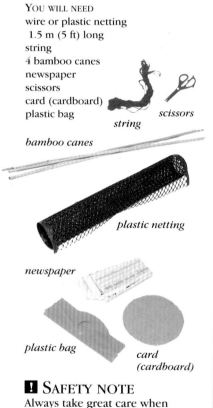

string
scissors
bamboo canes
plastic netting
newspaper
plastic bag
card (cardboard)

❗ SAFETY NOTE
Always take great care when using any sharp objects.

DID YOU KNOW?
A bin filled in spring will have rotted down and be ready to use by the end of summer, but a winter one will take longer.

1 Tie a piece of wire or plastic netting together with string to make a cylinder.

2 Thread at least 4 bamboo canes, evenly spaced through the netting. The canes should be at least 20 cm (8 in) longer than the height of the cylinder. Tie the canes to the net with string.

3 Stick the canes into the ground so they anchor the netting securely.

4 Line the bin well with plenty of sheets of old newspaper.

5 Start to fill with things like vegetable peelings, old tea bags and banana skins. Chop up garden clippings and put them in too.

6 Make a lid out of a piece of card (cardboard) and stick into a plastic bag to keep the rain out. When the bin is full leave it to rot down before you use it.

Fatty Feeders

Birds are very welcome visitors to gardens. Over the winter you can get them to come in really close to a window by hanging up one of these fatty feeders. Just make sure it is somewhere that you can spot the visitors. All kinds of birds that already live in or near your garden are just longing to get to know you better.

YOU WILL NEED
small bowl
selection of birdseed, nuts and fruit
lard (shortening)
small saucepan
small plastic pot
scissors
string
small stick

scissors

string

stick

plastic pot

lard (shortening)

nuts and fruit

1 Fill a small bowl full of peanuts, birdseed, apples and anything else you think the birds might fancy. Mix everything together thoroughly.

2 Melt about 100 g (4 oz/½ cup) of lard (shortening) in a small saucepan, then pour it over the nut mixture (this is probably enough to make two feeders).

3 Make a small hole in the bottom of the plastic pot and thread through one end of a long piece of string. Tie a small stick or piece of bamboo cane to the other end of the string.

4 Fill the pot with the fatty mixture. Pull the string through so the stick rests against the open end to make a perch. Leave it in a cool place to set.

5 When the fat has hardened, carefully pull off the plastic pot, and your feeder is ready to hang on a tree branch, bird table or windowsill.

Herby Vinegar

What a difference a sprig or two of herbs makes to a bottle of boring old vinegar! It looks much prettier and the hint of herbs gives it a more interesting flavour. It makes a great gift too.

YOU WILL NEED
sprigs of assorted herbs
pretty glass bottle with a cork top
cider or wine vinegar
label and pen

glass bottle with a cork top

label

pen

vinegar

herbs

1 Pick some herbs from the garden, look for perfect leaves without any marks or insect bites. Good herbs to use are rosemary, purple sage, thyme and marjoram.

2 Trim, wash and dry the herbs and put a selection of them in the bottle.

DID YOU KNOW?
Use your herb vinegar within two weeks, otherwise it will become poisonous.

3 Fill the bottle with cider or white wine vinegar. Put the top on securely.

4 Label the bottle. You can start to use the vinegar straight away.

Pineapple Plant

Pineapple tops will grow into handsome, spiky houseplants. Pineapples come from the tropics where they fruit easily, with just one pineapple growing out of the centre of each plant. There are reports of magnificent pineapple fruits being grown in English greenhouses 150 years ago, so you never know your luck!

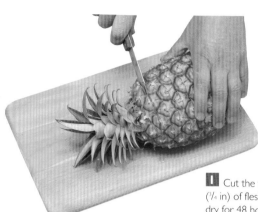

1 Cut the topknot off with about 2 cm (³/₄ in) of flesh and leave it on its side to dry for 48 hours.

YOU CAN USE
pineapple
knife
pebbles
flower pot about 10 cm (4 in)
 across the top
sand
potting compost (soil)
plastic bag
string

potting compost (soil)

string

pineapple

pebbles

sand

flower pot

knife

plastic bag

2 Put a layer of pebbles in the bottom of the pot for drainage.

3 Mix equal quantities of sand and potting compost (soil) together to make a light, well-draining mixture.

4 Fill the pot with the compost (soil) and sand mixture and press level lightly.

GARDENER'S TIP

After a week or two, untie the top of the bag to let in a bit of air. When you notice the leaves in the middle starting to grow again, it means you have successful rooting and the plastic bag can be removed. Don't forget to keep watering as the pineapple grows.

5 Put the pineapple top in position and cover over the fleshy part with the potting compost (soil).

6 Water in well and put the whole pot into a plastic bag tied at the top, to keep the air warm and moist, and put it on a warm windowsill.

! **SAFETY NOTE**
Always take great care when using any sharp objects.

Spring into Action

On misty, autumn (fall) days spring might seem a long time away, but gardeners have to think ahead. If you want a cheerful pot of flowers to greet you early next year, now is the time to get planting. There are hundreds of different types of spring flowering bulbs to choose from, and mixed and matched with forget-me-nots, daisies, pansies or wallflowers, you cannot go wrong. You might wonder how the tulips will find a gap among the other plants to grow, but they will find a way to push up their strong, sturdy stems.

YOU WILL NEED
large flower pot
small stones for drainage
potting compost (soil)
tulip bulbs
wallflowers
forget-me-nots, daisies or pansies

flower pot

forget-me-nots

wallflowers

stones

potting compost (soil)

tulip bulbs

1 Use the biggest pot that you have got and put a few stones over the hole in the bottom to stop the potting compost (soil) falling out.

2 Fill the pot two-thirds full with potting compost (soil).

3 Plant about 5 tulip bulbs, making sure they are the right way up with the pointed end on top.

4 Cover the bulbs over with handfuls of potting compost (soil).

5 Using your hands to make holes, plant 3 wallflowers evenly spaced out. If you dig up a tulip bulb by mistake, just pop it back in again.

6 Fill in any gaps with forget-me-nots, double daisies or pansies, or a mixture. Give all the plants a good watering.

GARDENER'S TIP

They will not need watering a lot over the autumn (fall) and winter but they will need some, so keep an eye on the pot and if it dries out, give it a good drink.

Monkey Nuts

Most of us like eating peanuts, but it is surprising how little most people know about the plant that they come from. In fact peanuts are not really nuts at all, but are related to peas and beans. The plant is quite small and lives for just one season. Its flowers bend down to the ground after they have been pollinated, and plant themselves in the soil where the fruit or "nuts" develop.

YOU WILL NEED
large flower pot – at least 12 cm
 (5 in) in diameter
potting compost (soil)
peanuts in their shells (unsalted)
cling film (plastic wrap)

*potting
compost (soil)*

peanuts

flower pot

*cling film
(plastic wrap)*

1 Fill a large pot with potting compost (soil) and press down lightly to make the surface level. Crack the peanuts across the middle with your fingers.

2 Plant the peanuts on their sides, putting in about 7-8 spaced evenly apart.

3 Cover them with about 2 cm (³/₄ in) of potting compost (soil) and water them well.

4 Cover the whole pot with cling film (plastic wrap) to keep them warm and moist and encourage them to grow. Remove the cling film (plastic wrap) when they have germinated, which should take about 2 weeks.

GARDENER'S TIP
Peanuts which have been roasted will not grow. Peanut plants will only produce fruit in very hot countries.

Some Pippy Ones

What is your favourite fruit - a juicy orange, a crunchy apple or perhaps a tangy lemon to make fresh lemonade? The good news is that all these fruits have pips (seeds), which could grow into plants. So instead of putting them into the dustbin (trash can), try planting them. You could grow interesting houseplants that will cost you nothing but pips (seeds) and patience.

YOU WILL NEED
orange and lemon pips (seeds)
small flower pot
potting compost (soil)

orange   *lemon*

flower pot

1 Save all the pips (seeds) you can when you are eating fruit.

2 Fill a small flower pot with potting compost (soil) and press down lightly to make the surface level. Plant the pips (seeds) by spacing them out evenly and pressing them into the compost (soil).

3 Then cover them over with about 1 cm (1/2 in) of potting compost. (soil).

4 Water them well. Put on a sunny windowsill.

GARDENER'S TIP
When they germinate move them into individual pots. Some seeds (pips) may take up to a month to germinate.

Glass Gardening

Welcome to the world of glass gardens, plants that live within a jar. This is a mini tropical rainforest, it does not need much watering because the water is recycled. Jars and bowls of almost all shapes and sizes can be transformed into a glass garden, so see what you can find. A large sweet (candy) jar does a first class job but I bet you don't get a chance to empty one of those very often!

You will need
gravel
glass bowl
charcoal
potting compost (soil)
selection of small houseplants
spoon and fork attached to
 pieces of cane to make
 long-handled tools for planting
plate for lid

potting compost (soil)

plate

glass bowl

charcoal

houseplants

fork

gravel

spoon

1 Put a generous layer of gravel in the bottom of the container.

2 Mix two handfuls of charcoal into the potting compost (soil), then fill the container one-third full.

3 Start to plant delicate plants that are normally quite difficult to grow indoors. This is a silver fern.

4 Then add an aluminium plant and a small African violet.

5 A polka-dot plant and some creeping moss completes the planting. Now give it a thoroughly good drink to start the water cycle off.

6 Put a plate or lid on top to close the glass garden.

Gardener's tip

By moving the top on and off, you can control the atmosphere inside. If water is running continuously down the sides, it is probably too wet, so take off the lid for a few days to let it dry out. Slight fogging collecting on the glass means the conditions are perfect – if there is no fogging, the conditions could be too dry and you will need to do some hand watering.

Did you know?

Water in a glass jar is recycled in much the same way as it is in the earth's atmosphere. Inside the jar water evaporates from the surface of the soil and from the plants themselves, but rather than rising to form high clouds in the atmosphere, it collects on the inside of the glass and runs down the sides (like rain), and as the plants are watered the cycle is complete.

Celebration Tree

There is something very special about planting a tree. It will live longer than us and grow much taller, so what better way to celebrate a new baby, a birthday or a family reunion? Trees are extremely important because they create the air that all living things breathe. Not everyone has room in their garden for a majestic oak or beech tree, but you could plant a smaller species such as a Whitebeam. This little tree has silvery, white undersides to the leaves and beautiful, scented white flowers followed by bright red fruits.

YOU WILL NEED
spade
sheet of plastic
fork
manure or garden compost
small tree
stake
hammer
2 tree ties

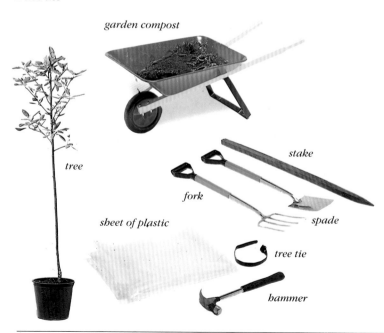

garden compost

tree

fork

sheet of plastic

stake

spade

tree tie

hammer

1 Remove the turf and dig a hole at least 7.5 cm (3 in) deeper than the depth of the pot which the tree is in, putting all the soil onto a sheet of plastic to keep the garden tidy.

2 Fork over the bottom of the hole and add a generous helping of manure or compost. This helps to feed the tree and will also help to hold water in the soil under its roots.

3 Take the tree out of its pot carefully and place it in position.

4 Put the stake in the hole close to the roots and hammer in place. The stake should be just below the first branch.

! SAFETY NOTE
Always take great care when using any sharp objects.

GARDENER'S TIP
If you cannot get special tree ties, use a pair of old tights (panty hose) instead, to stop the tree rubbing against the stake.

5 Start to put the soil back in the planting hole, firming it lightly and gently around the tree roots.

6 Fix two tree ties on securely, one at the bottom and one at the top of the stake. Finally, give it a really good drink to set it off on a long and healthy life.

GARDENER'S TIP
After about 3 years, when the tree is well established, the stake can be removed carefully.

Less Makes More

Plants that die down every winter but pop up again each spring are called border perennials. They can be expensive, but as they are often sold in quite large pots, it is possible to split them up into pieces and get perhaps three plants for the price of one.

This border perennial is called Pearl Everlasting. It has leaves which are covered with white hairs giving it a silvery appearance, and clusters of small starry flowers. The flower heads can be cut and dried – they keep perfectly.

YOU WILL NEED
good-sized pot of Pearl Everlasting
2 hand forks
trowel

Pearl
Everlasting

hand forks

1 Take the plant out of its pot and push two hand forks into the plant back to back, one in the middle and the other nearer the edge.

2 Pull them apart very carefully, gently splitting the plant into two pieces, one larger than the other.

3 Split the larger piece again and take off any damaged roots and loosen some of the others.

4 Plant each piece in a flower bed about 30 cm (12 in) apart. Water in thoroughly.

GARDENER'S TIP
You can also use this method for plants like Michaelmas daisies, marsh marigolds, bleeding hearts, day-lilies and lupins (lupines) among others.

Rock It

Part of the fascination of rock gardens is that it is possible to create a small piece of hillside or mountain in your own garden. Play around with the rocks until you are happy with their position and keep standing back a few paces to get a proper picture of the over all effect.

YOU WILL NEED
spade
gardening gloves
rocks
garden soil
trowel
alpine plants
grit

rocks

garden soil

grit

trowel

gardening gloves

alpine plants

1 Wearing gardening gloves, put the biggest rock in a hole that is deep enough to bury the bottom third. Lean the rock back slightly and press in firmly.

2 Arrange the next two biggest rocks either side of the first. Fill in the gaps with some garden soil. Use lots of soil so that a mound begins to form.

3 Put two or three more rocks on the next level, making sure they are secure. Then fill in with more soil.

4 Place a final rock on the top, making sure it is still one-third buried

5 Plant a collection of alpine plants among the rocks, putting a small handful of grit in the bottom of each planting hole – the soil on a hillside is much quicker draining than most garden soils and alpine plants don't like wet feet.

6 Cover the soil around the plants with a layer of grit, which gives it a natural finish and stops any water sitting in puddles around the plants.

Bird Table

Birds work very hard at finding enough food to eat, especially in the winter. To help them out and to make feathered friends who will visit you for years, put together this bird table and keep it stocked up with food such as birdseed, stale bread, fruit and bits of cheese. Once they start visiting the table they will come to rely on you, so always be on the look-out for scraps.

YOU WILL NEED
4 strips of wood, 27 cm
  (10 in) long
square piece of wood, 30 cm x
  30 cm (12 in x 12 in) and
  approximately 1 cm (in) thick
nails
hammer
varnish
paintbrush
screw-eyes
tall post or string

hammer

nails

screw-eyes

string

wood

! SAFETY NOTE
Always take great care when using a hammer.

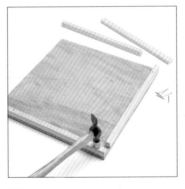

1 Nail the thin strips of wood around the edges of the square piece. Leave a gap at each corner to allow the rain water to drain away.

2 Varnish and leave to dry. Screw a few screw-eyes to the underneath of the board. You can hang food from these afterwards.

3 Fix to the top of a tall post by hammering two or three nails through the middle of the board and into the post below. Ask an adult to hammer the table firmly into the ground.

4 Alternatively, screw in one screw-eye to each corner on the upper surface. Tie on two loops of string by knotting the ends through the screw-eyes. Then you can hang the table (feeder) from a suitable tree or hook. A hanging table is best if cats are a problem in your garden.

Making a Hide

Most wild animals are scared when they see people and quickly get out of sight, but if you are camouflaged and keep quiet and still they won't know you are there and you can get a really good look. Build a hide near a bird table, leave it up for a few hours until the birds get used to it, then crawl in, wait, and watch them as they feed, you can see them but they can't see you!

YOU WILL NEED
4 long and 4 short bamboo canes
string
scissors
large dark cloth
large safety pins

cloth

bamboo canes

string

safety pins

scissors

1 Push four long canes into the ground in a square shape.

2 Use pieces of string to tie the remaining shorter canes in a square round the top.

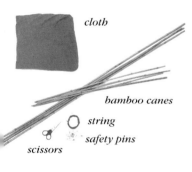

3 Cover with the cloth. If the bamboo canes are wobbly, push them further into the ground.

GARDENER'S TIP
It is important that the cloth you use is a dark colour so that it blends into the background.

4 Use the safety pins to join the sides together, leaving spaces big enough crawl in and to look through. When you are inside remember to be very still and quiet or you will frighten away the animals you are trying to watch.

Piggy-back Plant

Plants have very clever ways of making new plants. Many produce thousands of seeds each year in the hope that a few of them will land on fertile ground. The piggy-back plant, however, grows baby plantlets which it carries on its back in the middle of the leaf. If you pin these down onto a pot of potting compost (soil), they will make their own roots very quickly.

! SAFETY NOTE
Always take great care when using any sharp objects.

YOU WILL NEED
penknife
piggy-back plant
small flower pot
potting compost (soil)
small piece of wire
plastic bag
string

piggy-back plant

plastic bag

string

wire

flower pot and compost

1 Using the penknife, cut off a large, healthy leaf with a plantlet in the middle.

2 Fill a small pot with potting compost (soil). Lay the leaf on top, fixing it in place by pinning it down with a U-shaped piece of wire.

3 Water the pot thoroughly.

4 Put the pot into a plastic bag and tie the top with string.

GARDENER'S TIP
It will take 2 or 3 weeks to root. You can tell when it has rooted, because the leaves in the middle will start to grow and develop. It may need watering again during this time – if the pot feels light, water it.

Crazy Grass-head

Crazy grass-heads make great mates to have lounging around on your windowsill. Grow a head of long, wild green hair for a cool dude, or keep it trimmed regularly and looking neat and tidy. They cost practically nothing to make and are very original presents for your friends, if you can bear to give them away.

GARDENER'S TIP
The bottom of the sock sucks up water from the paper cup. Never let it go thirsty or the hair will wilt! Keep it on a windowsill that gets plenty of daylight.

YOU WILL NEED
old sock or pair of tights
 (panty hose)
scissors
grass seed
potting compost (soil)
cotton thread
elastic band
pieces of felt
fabric glue
paper cup

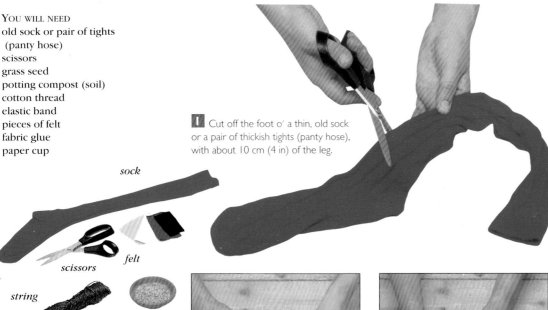

1 Cut off the foot o' a thin, old sock or a pair of thickish tights (panty hose), with about 10 cm (4 in) of the leg.

sock

scissors *felt*

string

cotton thread

grass seed

fabric glue

paper cup

potting compost (soil)

2 Put a generous handful of grass seed in the end of the toe and press it down in a thick layer.

❗ SAFETY NOTE
Always take great care when using any sharp objects.

3 Fill up the toe with potting compost (soil) pressing down each handful firmly, so you end up with a good-sized head that is quite solid. It can be any size you want but the bigger the better.

4 Knot the end like a balloon, or tie it firmly with string or strong cotton thread. Make the nose by pulling out a wodge in the middle and fixing an elastic band around the bottom.

5 Cut out the eyes, mouth and even a beard or moustache from the felt. Stick them in place using fabric glue. Leave to dry overnight. Next morning sit the head on top of a paper cup filled with water.

Hanging Houseplants

The inch plants (Tradescantia or Wandering Jew) are perhaps the most popular of all hanging plants, being very easy to look after and happy-go-lucky. There are many different types, all with slightly different leaf colours but one thing they all share is that they are very easy to grow from cuttings – they will even root in a glass of water.

YOU WILL NEED
penknife
inch plant
glass of water
small flower pot
potting compost (soil)

! SAFETY NOTE
Always take great care when using any sharp objects.

inch plant

penknife

potting compost (soil)

glass of water

1 Using a penknife, cut off one of the tips of the plant about 5 cm (2 in) long.

2 Remove some of the lower leaves, leaving 3 or 4 at the top.

3 Put the cutting into a glass of water and put on a warm (but not too sunny) windowsill.

4 After a couple of weeks some white roots will have grown. Move the cutting to its own little pot of potting compost (soil). When it has grown another 5 cm (2 in) nip off the very tip of it. This is called pinching out and helps the plant to grow bushy instead of spindly.

Name It

Every time you sow some seeds, don't forget to stick a label in the pot. Many flowers look the same as seedlings, so if you don't label them, you could end up with monster sunflowers in a window box!

YOU WILL NEED
large plastic yoghurt pot
scissors
ruler
ballpoint pen

yoghurt pot

ballpoint pen

ruler

scissors

1 Cut lengthways down the side of a large yoghurt pot, then carefully cut out the bottom.

2 Open the side out flat and cut off the rim. Using a ruler and ballpoint pen, draw lines about 2 cm (³/₄ in) apart.

3 Cut along the lines with the scissors.

4 Cut a tapered point at one end to stick into the pot or soil. Now your labels are ready to write on.

! SAFETY NOTE
Always take great care when using any sharp objects.

Wonderful Worms

Worms are truly wonderful creatures that we often take for granted. They keep the soil healthy by making channels for air and water and by eating plant remains. A wormery is an excellent way of making potting compost from kitchen scraps. It is on a smaller scale than a compost bin and provides a richer material which can be used for potting up plants. The type of worms that live most happily in a wormery are not earthworms which you find in the soil, but tiger worms which you can buy from most fishing tackle shops.

YOU WILL NEED
hand drill
small dustbin (trash can)
gravel
newspaper
potting compost (soil)
tiger worms
vegetable peelings

dustbin (trash can)

gravel

potting compost (soil)

vegetable peelings

tiger worms *hand drill*

newspaper

1 Drill two rows of drainage holes 2.5 cm (1 in) up from the bottom of a small dustbin (trash can), plus a row of air holes around the top.

! SAFETY NOTE
Always take great care when using any type of drill.

3 Cover with a layer of wet newspaper, which stops the compost (soil) falling through onto the gravel.

2 Put a 10 cm (4-in) layer of gravel in the bottom.

4 Then add a 10 cm (4-in) layer of potting compost (soil).

5 Now add a good handful of tiger worms, use gloves if you like!

6 Add a thin layer of vegetable peelings and cover everything with a thick layer of newspaper. It will take a couple of weeks for the worms to settle into their new home. Don't add more vegetable peelings until the worms have started to work on the previous batch and only add a thin layer at a time.

DID YOU KNOW?

Worms' favourite foods are banana skins, tea-bags, carrot and potato peelings, and all greens. They are not very keen on orange or lemon skins so it is best to leave them out.

Potty over Plants

Painted pots are cheap, fun to make and very, very useful. They are also the perfect way to show off your gardening triumphs. I have used clay pots which are quite classy but plastic, or even tin, would work well too.

YOU WILL NEED
small clay flower pot
white primer paint and ceramic paints
paintbrush
pens
scissors
thick paper for stencils
scouring sponge

scouring sponge

thick paper

pen

scissors

ceramic paints

flower pot

white primer paint

paintbrush

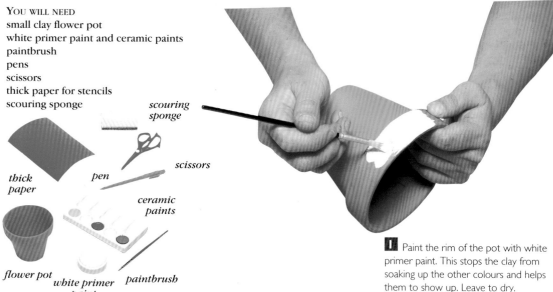

1 Paint the rim of the pot with white primer paint. This stops the clay from soaking up the other colours and helps them to show up. Leave to dry.

2 Draw simple leaf and petal patterns on a piece of paper.

3 Cut the patterns out carefully to make stencils.

4 Cut a scouring sponge into small pieces with the scissors.

5 Place the stencil on the pot rim. Dip the corners of the sponge pieces into the ceramic paints and dab lightly on the cut-out pattern. Lift the paper off carefully and work around the pot.

6 Finish the details, like flower centres or stalks with a paintbrush.

Happy Christmas Tree

If you buy a Christmas tree with roots on and look after it properly, it can last for years. The tree in the photograph is 5 years old and still going strong! The most important thing is not to let it get too hot and dry because it would really rather be outside in the winter snow and ice than in your cozy living room.

YOU WILL NEED
Christmas tree with roots on
a large pot
potting compost (soil)
plate for pot to stand on
watering can
Christmas decorations

Christmas tree

large pot   *potting compost (soil)*   *watering can*

1 As soon as you buy the tree, move it into a larger pot so there is at least a 2 cm (³/₄ in) gap between the roots and the sides of the pot. Fill the gap with compost (soil) and press down firmly.

GARDENER'S TIP
To brighten the tree up for the rest of the year, plant some flowers like pansies and fuchsias around the bottom.

2 Put the tree in a position where you can enjoy looking at it, but where it is cool, well away from fires or radiators. Find a large plate for the pot to stand in and give the tree a good drink of water.

3 Choose Christmas decorations which fit the size of the tree.

4 When Christmas is over, put the tree in its pot back outside as soon as possible, in a sheltered corner away from any strong winds.

Hyacinths for Christmas

Every year I have a competition with myself to try to get bowls of sweetly scented hyacinths in flower for Christmas. The secret is to plant them as soon as you see the bulbs for sale in garden centres at the end of the summer. Buy the largest bulbs you can and choose those that are described as "prepared". This means that they have been tricked by the grower into thinking that it is spring and time for them to wake up and start growing.

YOU WILL NEED
pretty pot
pebbles
potting compost (soil)
hyacinth bulb
newspaper

potting compost (soil)

pot

pebbles

hyacinth bulb

newspaper

1 Fill a pretty pot, or decorate one yourself and put a few pebbles in the bottom for drainage.

2 Fill the pot half-full with potting compost (soil).

3 Plant the hyacinth bulb, putting some compost around it but leaving the top of the bulb, which is called the nose, just showing. Water the pot well.

4 Cover the pot with a thick layer of newspaper to keep out the light. Put it somewhere cool like a shed or unheated room for 6 weeks. During this time water once or twice. After 6 weeks, take off the newspaper, put the pot on a windowsill, and wait for the flowers to come.

GATESIDE PRIMARY
FIFE

Stems, 13
Strawberries: growing, 52
    window box, in, 28
Succulents, 47
Summer squash, 40
Sunflowers, 30
Sunny spot, plants for, 24
Sweet peas, 76